Our Favorite
Sauces, Marinades
& Rubs

Smoky Mountain Barbecue Sauce is scrumptious
on grilled chicken... just add corn on the cob
and your meal is complete!

Smoky Mountain Barbecue Sauce

Makes about 2-1/2 cups

1/4 c. oil
1/2 c. onion, chopped
1 clove garlic, minced
1 c. tomato purée
1 c. water

1/4 c. brown sugar, packed
1/4 c. cider vinegar
1 T. chili powder
3 whole cloves
1 bay leaf

Heat oil in a skillet over medium heat. Add onion and garlic; cook until onion is clear. Stir in remaining ingredients. Simmer until brown sugar is dissolved and sauce has thickened, stirring occasionally. Discard bay leaf and cloves. Cover and refrigerate if not used immediately.

Serving tip:

Brush sauce over ribs, chicken, chops or burgers while grilling.

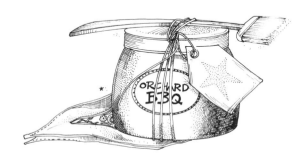

Fill Mason jars with your own special savory sauce to give
as a take-home gift. Tie on a recipe card and a BBQ brush
with a bit of jute...cookout guests will love it!

Good-on-Anything BBQ Sauce

Makes 4 cups

2 c. catsup
1 c. water
1/4 c. cider vinegar
1/4 c. molasses
1/2 c. brown sugar, packed
1/4 c. sugar

1 T. yellow mustard
1 t. dry mustard
1 t. onion powder
1 t. chili powder
2 to 3 cloves garlic, minced

In a saucepan over medium heat, whisk all ingredients together. Cook until mixture starts to bubble and thickens slightly. Use immediately or refrigerate up to 2 days.

Serving tip:

Brush this versatile sauce over the meat of your choice while grilling or broiling.

The true essentials of a feast are only food and fun.

-Oliver Wendell Holmes, Sr.

Tangy BBQ Chicken Sauce

Makes about 2-1/2 cups

1 c. brewed coffee
1 c. catsup
1/2 c. sugar

1/2 c. Worcestershire sauce
1/4 c. cider vinegar
1/8 t. pepper

Combine all ingredients in a saucepan over medium heat. Bring to a boil; reduce heat to low. Simmer, uncovered, for 30 to 35 minutes until thickened, stirring occasionally.

Serving tip:

Grill 8 chicken thighs and/or drumsticks as desired, brushing with sauce as chicken cooks.

Make the kids' table fun! Use a sheet of butcher paper for the tablecloth. Place a flowerpot filled with markers, crayons and stickers in the middle...they'll have a blast!

White BBQ Sauce

Makes about 1-3/4 cups

1-1/2 c. mayonnaise
1/4 c. white wine vinegar
1 T. coarse pepper
1 T. spicy brown mustard

2 t. prepared horseradish
1 t. sugar
1 t. salt
1 clove garlic, minced

Stir together all ingredients until well blended. Use immediately, or keep refrigerated in an airtight container up to one week.

Serving tip:

Grill 3 pounds chicken pieces as desired. At serving time, drizzle chicken with White BBQ Sauce.

If it's a warm spring or summer day, consider enjoying dinner outside, Italian style! Set the table with touches of green, white and red...the colors of the Italian flag are ideal paired with bunches of grapes and Italian music playing in the background.

Easy-Peasy Bolognese Sauce

Makes about 10 cups, or 10 to 12 servings

1/4 lb. bacon, chopped
1 T. olive oil
1 c. onion, minced
1 c. carrots, peeled and minced
3/4 c. celery, minced
2 lbs. lean ground beef

salt and pepper to taste
1/4 c. white wine or chicken broth
2 28-oz. cans crushed tomatoes
3 bay leaves
1/2 c. half-and-half
1/4 c. fresh parsley, chopped

Cook bacon in a large skillet over medium heat until just crisp. Add olive oil, onion, carrots and celery; cook until vegetables are tender, about 5 minutes. Add beef; season with salt and pepper. Continue cooking until beef is almost completely browned, about 10 minutes; drain. Add wine or broth; cook for 3 to 4 minutes. Transfer beef mixture to a slow cooker; stir in tomatoes with juice and bay leaves. Cover and cook on low setting for 6 hours; season again with salt and pepper. Discard bay leaves; stir in half-and-half and parsley just before serving.

Serving tip:
Use this delicious sauce in your favorite pasta or lasagna recipe.

Don't pass up a pretty sugar bowl just because it has lost its lid...turn it into a sweet flower vase. Slip a block of floral foam inside and arrange short-stemmed marigolds or zinnias in the foam.

Stacie's Spaghetti Sauce

Makes 4 to 6 servings

1 onion, chopped
1 green pepper, chopped
1 T. olive oil
1 lb. ground beef
28-oz. can diced tomatoes

15-oz. can tomato sauce
6-oz. can tomato paste
1 T. Worcestershire sauce
1 t. garlic powder
salt and pepper to taste

In a large skillet or stockpot over medium heat, sauté onion and green pepper in olive oil until tender. Add beef and cook until browned; drain. Stir in tomatoes with juice and remaining ingredients. Reduce heat to low; cover and simmer for at least one hour, stirring occasionally.

Serving tip:

Use immediately with your favorite pasta or spoon into a plastic zipping bag and freeze for later.

Some yummy ways to enjoy pesto sauce...serve with meat or fish. Stir into hot pasta dishes or vegetables. Add to sour cream or mayonnaise to make a scrumptious dressing.

Fresh Herb Pesto Sauce   *Makes about 1-1/2 cups*

2 c. fresh herb leaves like
  basil, parsley, oregano,
  mint, tarragon or sage,
  coarsely chopped
1 c. pine nuts or chopped walnuts,
  toasted if desired

6 cloves garlic, chopped
1/2 c. plus 1 T. olive oil, divided
1/2 t. salt
3/4 c. grated Parmesan or
  Romano cheese

In a blender, combine herbs, nuts, garlic, 1/2 cup olive oil and salt. Process until smooth, adding a little more oil if needed to make blending easier. Transfer to a bowl; stir in grated cheese. Cover and refrigerate up to 3 days, or spoon into ice cube trays and freeze for later use.

Serving tip:
Spread pesto sauce on toasted baguettes for a quick appetizer.

Steam vegetables to keep their fresh-picked taste...it's simple.
Bring 1/2 inch of water to a boil in a saucepan and add cut-up
veggies. Cover and cook to desired tenderness, about 3 to
5 minutes. A quick toss with a little butter or olive oil
and they're ready to enjoy.

Portabella-Basil Alfredo Sauce *Makes 8 to 10 servings*

1 T. olive oil	1-1/2 t. dried basil
5 portabella mushrooms, chopped	8-oz. pkg. cream cheese, cubed
3 c. milk	3-oz. pkg. cream cheese, cubed
1-1/2 t. garlic salt	1-1/2 c. grated Parmesan cheese

Heat olive oil in a large skillet over medium heat. Sauté mushrooms until tender, about 5 minutes; drain any extra liquid from pan. Add milk and garlic salt to skillet; heat just to boiling. Stir in basil and both packages of cream cheese. Reduce heat to low; cook, stirring constantly, until cream cheese is melted. Stir in Parmesan cheese; cook over low heat just until melted.

Serving tip:

Serve over your favorite cooked fettuccine...try spinach pasta for a nice contrast with the white sauce.

A range of cooking times is often given on packages of pasta. The first cooking time is for al dente (firm to the bite) and the second cooking time is for a softer pasta. You choose!

Jezebel Raisin Sauce

Makes about 2 cups

1 c. sugar
1/2 c. water
8-oz. jar currant jelly
1 c. raisins, chopped
2 T. vinegar
1 T. Worcestershire sauce

1/2 t. salt
1/8 t. pepper
1/4 t. cinnamon
1/8 t. ground cloves
1/8 t. ground ginger

Combine sugar and water in a large saucepan over medium heat. Bring to a boil; boil for 2 minutes, stirring until sugar dissolves. Add remaining ingredients; reduce heat to medium and cook until blended. Serve immediately, or cool and refrigerate up to 3 days. Reheat before serving.

Serving tip:

Serve this Southern favorite hot, spooned over baked ham, pork roast or roast turkey.

Family favorites like homemade salsa, jams & jellies are perfect hostess gifts...simply tie on a bow and gift tag!

Texas Green Sauce

Makes about 5 cups

4 avocados, pitted, peeled
    and chopped
16-oz. container sour cream
10-oz. can diced tomatoes with
    green chiles
4-oz. can diced green chiles

3-oz. pkg. cream cheese, cubed
    and softened
1 T. garlic powder
2 t. salt
1 t. lemon juice

Combine all ingredients in a blender; process until smooth. Transfer to
a covered container; refrigerate up to 3 days.

Serving tip:

Serve with your favorite tortilla chips, or spooned onto chalupas
or taquitos.

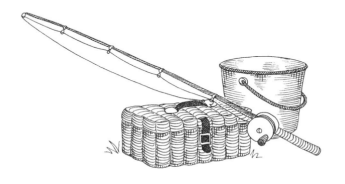

If people concentrated on the really important things in life,
there'd be a shortage of fishing poles.

-Doug Larson

Cucumber Dill Sauce

1 cucumber, peeled and divided	zest and juice of 1 lemon
8-oz. container sour cream	1 t. sugar
1 T. fresh dill, chopped, or 1 t. dill weed	salt and pepper to taste

Grate 1/4 of the cucumber into a bowl; set aside. Cut remaining cucumber into 1/2-inch cubes and add to grated cucumber. Stir in remaining ingredients; mix thoroughly. Cover and chill until ready to serve, about 30 minutes.

Serving tip:

A cool, refreshing sauce that's especially tasty spooned over shrimp, salmon and other fish, even grilled vegetables.

Use a grill basket to cook small pieces of meat, fish and veggies...they won't fall through the grate and are much easier to turn for even cooking.

Lemon-Garlic Grilling Sauce

Makes 3/4 cup

1/4 c. lemon juice
1/4 c. butter, melted
1/4 c. olive oil

1 T. green hot pepper sauce
3 cloves garlic, minced

Combine all ingredients in a bowl, mix well. Use immediately.

Serving tip:

Brush sauce onto fish, seafood, chicken or vegetables while grilling.

Pack up your fishing gear and head to a peaceful lake or shady riverbank. Even if you don't catch any fish, you'll enjoy a day of relaxing fun!

Fresh Tartar Sauce

Makes about 1-1/2 cups

1 c. mayonnaise-style
   salad dressing
1/2 c. sweet pickle relish

2 T. onion, chopped
1 T. lemon juice

In a bowl, mix together all ingredients. Use immediately, or cover and refrigerate up to one week.

Serving tip:

Serve with your favorite fried or grilled fish.

Turn your favorite sliced or shredded pork, beef
or chicken barbecue into party food. Serve up
bite-size sandwiches on slider buns. Fun!

Ruby Sauce

Serves 4 to 6

1 c. brown sugar, packed
1 c. sugar
1 c. cider vinegar
1 t. ground ginger
1 t. cinnamon
1 t. allspice
1 t. paprika

1/2 t. ground cloves
1/2 t. red pepper flakes
1/2 t. salt
1/8 t. pepper
2 onions, finely chopped
4 c. rhubarb, finely chopped

Combine all ingredients except onions and rhubarb in a large saucepan over medium heat. Bring to a simmer. Stir in onions and rhubarb; reduce heat to medium-low. Cook for 45 minutes to one hour, stirring occasionally, until thickened and rhubarb is tender. Serve immediately, cover and refrigerate up to 3 days.

Serving tip:

Serve this unusual fruity sauce with grilled chicken, grilled ribs or pulled pork.

Remove grilled steak to a platter and let stand for
10 to 15 minutes before slicing and serving...
it'll be nice and juicy!

Chimichurri Sauce

1-1/2 c. fresh flat-leaf parsley, packed
3/4 c. extra-virgin olive oil
3 T. white wine vinegar

2 T. fresh oregano, chopped
6 cloves garlic, quartered
1/4 t. red pepper flakes
salt and pepper to taste

Combine all ingredients in a food processor; process until smooth. Use immediately, or refrigerate up to 4 hours; bring to room temperature at serving time.

Serving tip:

Serve this traditional green herb sauce from Argentina with grilled beef, chicken or fish.

Foil packet dinners go hand-in-hand with any cookout. Combine
potato and onion slices with a dash of paprika, garlic salt and pepper;
drizzle with olive oil. Place in a square of heavy-duty aluminum foil,
bring edges together to seal. Grill over medium heat for
25 minutes, or until potatoes are tender. Top servings with
a dollop of sour cream and snipped chives. Yum!

Spicy Hot Dog & Burger Sauce Makes about 5 cups

1 lb. ground beef, browned
   and drained
8-oz. can tomato sauce
2 c. water
1-1/2 T. Worcestershire sauce
1 T. prepared horseradish
1 t. hot pepper sauce

1 T. dried, minced onion
1 T. chili powder
1 t. dried oregano
1 t. cayenne pepper
1/8 t. nutmeg
1/8 t. salt

In a stockpot, combine all ingredients. Cover and simmer over low heat for 30 minutes, stirring occasionally. May also be prepared in a slow cooker; cover and cook on low setting for 3 to 4 hours, until hot and bubbly. Serve immediately, or cover and refrigerate up to 3 days. Reheat before serving.

Serving tip:

Spoon onto grilled hot dogs and burgers in buns for a real "take me out to the ballgame" meal.

Even an old boot tastes good if it is cooked over charcoal.

-Italian Proverb

Hank's Hot Sauce

1 lb. lean ground beef
1 T. Worcestershire sauce
1 T. chili powder
1 T. paprika

1 T. allspice
1-1/2 t. cayenne pepper, or to taste
1 t. garlic salt
1 t. onion salt

Crumble uncooked beef into a medium saucepan; add enough water to cover beef. Add remaining ingredients; bring to a boil over medium heat. Reduce heat to medium-low. Simmer for about one hour, stirring occasionally to break up beef. Serve immediately, or keep refrigerated and reheat at serving time.

Serving tip:

This sauce has a nice flavor served on hot dogs and hamburgers, and isn't extremely spicy.

A fun and simple meal...try a chili dog bar! Along with cooked
hot dogs and buns, set out some chili sauce, shredded cheese,
sauerkraut, chopped onions and your favorite condiments.
Kids love it, and it's easy on the hostess.

Classic Coney Sauce

Makes enough sauce for
about 20 hot dogs

3 lbs. lean ground beef, browned
   and drained
28-oz. can tomato purée
1 c. onion, chopped
2 T. chili powder

1-1/2 T. mustard
1-1/2 T. Worcestershire sauce
1 T. salt
1 T. pepper
1 t. garlic powder

Combine all ingredients in a slow cooker. Cover and cook on high setting
for 3 hours, stirring occasionally. Turn heat to low setting to keep warm
for serving.

Serving tip:

Makes enough for a tailgating party, block party or get-together. Serve
right from the slow cooker!

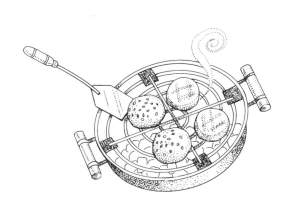

Buns for hot dogs and burgers just taste better toasted...
they won't get soggy either. Simply butter buns lightly and place
on a hot grill for 30 seconds to one minute, until toasted to taste.

Cindy's Special Sauce

Makes 4 cups

1/4 c. butter
1 onion, chopped
24-oz. bottle catsup

1/2 c. white vinegar
3/4 c. brown sugar, packed

Melt butter in a saucepan over medium heat. Add onion and cook until tender, about 5 minutes. Stir in remaining ingredients. Simmer for 5 minutes, or until brown sugar dissolves, stirring often. Use immediately, or cover and refrigerate up to 3 days.

Serving tip:

Delicious on charcoal-grilled burgers, steamed hot dogs, French fries and more!

Make a scrumptious brownie sundae! Place a brownie in a dessert dish and top with a scoop of vanilla ice cream. Top it off with some warm Grandma Bevy's Hot Fudge Sauce. Yum!

Grandma Bevy's
Hot Fudge Sauce

Makes about 1-1/2 cups

1 c. sugar
2 T. baking cocoa
1/2 c. half-and-half

2 T. light corn syrup
1 T. butter, diced
1/2 t. vanilla extract

Combine sugar and cocoa in a saucepan; stir in half-and-half. Add corn syrup and butter; mix well. Bring to a boil over medium heat, stirring constantly. Reduce heat to medium-low; simmer for 10 minutes without stirring. Remove from heat; stir in vanilla. Tastes best when served immediately, but may be refrigerated and reheated when ready to serve.

Serving tip:

Drizzle over homemade cream puffs or scoops of your favorite ice cream...yummy!

For delicious apple desserts, some of the best apple varieties
are Granny Smith, Gala and Jonathan as well as old-timers
like Rome Beauty, Northern Spy & Winesap.

Warm Caramel Sauce

1/2 c. brown sugar, packed	1 c. water
2 T. all-purpose flour	1 T. butter
1/8 t. salt	1/4 t. vanilla extract

Combine brown sugar, flour and salt in a small saucepan. Gradually add water; stir until smooth. Cook and stir over medium heat until mixture comes to a boil. Cook for one to 2 minutes, until thickened. Remove from heat; stir in butter and vanilla.

Serving tip:

Easy to stir up at the last minute! Serve warm drizzled over a slice of cheesecake, your favorite apple cake or vanilla ice cream. Or use as a dipping sauce for crisp apple slices.

Mix up marinades an hour or so before you need 'em.
Refrigerate to let the flavors blend together.

Terrific Teriyaki Marinade *Makes about 1/2 cup*

1/4 c. soy sauce	1 T. red wine vinegar
2 T. oil	1 clove garlic, minced
2 T. honey	1 t. ground ginger

Whisk all ingredients together in a bowl. Use immediately.

Serving tip:

Place one pound favorite grilling steak or boneless chicken breasts in a plastic zipping bag. Pour marinade over meat; seal bag and turn to coat well. Refrigerate for at least 3 hours, turning bag several times to coat both sides. Drain, discarding any excess sauce; grill or broil meat as desired.

Fill uniquely shaped bottles from Grandma's pantry with
herb vinegars...you can even tuck in a fresh sprig of herbs
or herb blossoms. They'll sparkle on a windowsill.

All-Purpose Meat Marinade

Makes about one cup

1/2 c. oil
1/4 c. soy sauce
1/4 c. red wine vinegar
2 T. lemon juice
1 T. Worcestershire sauce

1 T. Dijon mustard
1 T. dried parsley
1 clove garlic, pressed
1/2 t. salt
1/2 t. pepper

Whisk all ingredients together. Use immediately.

Serving tip:

Place 4 to 6 serving-size pieces of chicken, beef, pork or fish in a plastic freezer bag or shallow dish. Add marinade; turn to coat well. Refrigerate or freeze until ready to prepare. Drain; bring marinade to a boil in a small saucepan. Grill meat as desired, brushing occasionally with marinade.

Tie up a bunch of fragrant herbs with jute or raffia
to use as a basting brush while grilling.

Jamaican Marinade

Makes enough marinade for 2 pounds chicken

1/3 c. olive oil
3 T. white vinegar
1-1/2 T. lime juice
1 T. sugar
1/4 c. green onions, minced
1 jalapeño pepper, seeded and
    chopped

2 cloves garlic, minced
1 t. dried thyme
3/4 t. allspice
1/2 t. cinnamon
1/2 t. salt
cayenne pepper to taste

Combine all ingredients in a bowl; mix well and use immediately.

Serving tip:

Place 2 pounds of chicken pieces in a large plastic zipping bag; pour marinade over chicken. Seal bag; turn to coat well. Refrigerate for 2 to 3 hours before grilling, turning bag occasionally. Drain; discard marinade and grill chicken as desired.

Crisp coleslaw pairs well with grilled fish. Perk up
your favorite coleslaw with some mandarin oranges
or pineapple tidbits for a delicious change.

Sweet & Easy Salmon Marinade

Makes enough marinade for 4 salmon fillets

2 T. butter
2 T. brown sugar, packed
1 to 2 cloves garlic, minced

1 T. lemon juice
2 t. soy sauce
1/2 t. pepper

Combine all ingredients in a small saucepan. Cook and stir over medium heat until brown sugar is dissolved; cool before using.

Serving tip:

Place 4 salmon fillets in a baking pan; pour cooled marinade over top. Let stand for 10 to 15 minutes. Remove salmon from pan and set aside; bring marinade to a boil in a small saucepan. Spray grill with non-stick vegetable spray; grill salmon over hot coals for 4 to 5 minutes per side side, basting occasionally with marinade.

Before marinating chicken, reserve some marinade in
a plastic squeeze bottle for easy basting...how clever!

Lemon-Lime Marinade

*Makes enough marinade
for 2 pounds chicken*

1/2 c. brown sugar, packed
3 T. Dijon mustard
1/4 c. cider vinegar
juice of one lime

juice of one lemon
6 T. olive oil
pepper to taste

Whisk ingredients together in a bowl until brown sugar dissolves.
Use immediately.

Serving tip:

Add 2 pounds chicken pieces to a large plastic zipping bag; pour marinade
over chicken. Seal bag and turn to coat chicken. Refrigerate overnight,
turning bag occasionally. Drain, discarding marinade; grill or broil chicken
as desired.

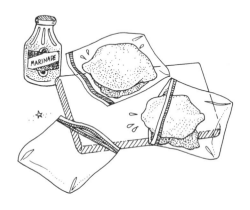

Alongside sticky finger foods like barbecued ribs and chicken wings, set out a basket of washcloths, moistened with lemon-scented water and warmed briefly in the microwave. Guests will thank you!

Wing-Ding-Wonder Marinade

Makes 1-1/2 cups

1 c. oil
1/2 c. soy sauce
1 T. lemon juice

1 t. ground ginger
4 cloves garlic, minced

Whisk all ingredients together; use immediately, or cover and refrigerate up to 3 days.

Serving tip:

This marinade is great with beef, pork, salmon and of course, chicken wings. Marinade one to 2 pounds meat for several hours to overnight; grill or broil as desired.

A diner-themed dinner is fun for the whole family.
Make placemats from vintage maps, roll up flatware
in paper napkins and serve catsup & mustard
from plastic squeeze bottles.

Hawaiian Chicken Marinade   *Makes about 1-1/4 cups*

1/2 c. pineapple juice
1/2 c. soy sauce
1/4 c. canola oil
1 T. brown sugar, packed

2 t. ground ginger
1 t. garlic powder
1 t. dry mustard
1/4 t. pepper

In a small saucepan, stir together all ingredients. Bring to a boil over medium heat; reduce heat and simmer for 5 minutes. Cool slightly; use immediately.

Serving tip:

Pour marinade over 1-1/2 to 2 pounds chicken pieces in a shallow dish; turn to coat. Cover and refrigerate for several hours. Drain; bring marinade to a boil in a small saucepan. Grill or bake chicken as desired, brushing with marinade. For a delicious addition, brush pineapple rings with marinade and grill or bake alongside chicken.

Heat tortillas right on the grill, turning when lightly browned.
Wrap hot tortillas in aluminum foil to keep them warm.

Fajita Steak Marinade   *Makes about 3-1/4 cups*

2 c. pineapple juice
1/4 c. lime juice
1 c. soy sauce

2 T. ground cumin
1-1/2 t. garlic, minced

Whisk together all ingredients in a bowl until smooth. Use immediately, or cover and refrigerate up to 2 days.

Serving tip:

Place 2 to 3 pounds beef flank or skirt steak in a large plastic zipping bag; set aside. Pour over steak; seal bag and turn to coat. Refrigerate for 4 to 6 hours, turning bag occasionally. Drain; discard marinade. Place steak on an oiled grill over medium-high heat. Grill to desired doneness, about 3 to 4 minutes per side; remove to a cutting board and cool slightly before slicing. Serve steak with warmed tortillas, sautéed sliced peppers, tomatoes and other fajita fixings.

Mix up some chili salt to sprinkle on hot buttered corn on the cob! Just combine 4 teaspoons chili powder with 2 teaspoons kosher salt in a shaker.

Pork Chop Marinade for Grilling

Serves 4

3 T. soy sauce
1 T. brown sugar, packed
2 cloves garlic, minced

1 t. ground coriander
1 t. pepper

Stir together marinade ingredients in a bowl; use immediately or refrigerate until ready to use.

Serving tip:

Place 4 thick butterflied pork chops in a large plastic zipping bag. Pour marinade over pork chops; turn to coat. Seal bag and refrigerate for 2 to 4 hours, turning bag occasionally. Drain, discarding marinade. Grill chops for 5 minutes per side, or until juices no long run pink.

Revive the drive-in movie tradition in your own backyard!
Call a local camera or rental store for a video projector...
simply hook it to a DVD player and project your favorite
movie on a big white sheet or painter's cloth. Sure to be a hit!

Hunk o' Steak Pineapple Marinade   *Serves 6 to 8*

2 c. olive oil
1 onion, chopped
1/2 c. red steak sauce
1/2 c. Worcestershire sauce
20-oz. can pineapple chunks

2 c. regular or non-alcoholic beer
1 c. white wine or beef broth
2 T. granulated garlic
1 T. seasoned salt

In a large saucepan over medium heat, combine olive oil, onion and sauces. Cook, stirring occasionally, for 5 to 10 minutes. Add pineapple with juice and remaining ingredients. Simmer an additional 5 to 10 minutes; let cool. Use immediately, or cover and refrigerate until ready to use.

Serving tip:

Place 3 to 4 pounds beef flank steak in a shallow glass dish. Pour marinade with pineapple over steak. Cover and refrigerate for 8 hours to 2 days, turning steak occasionally. Drain, discarding marinade. Place pineapple chunks on skewers. Grill steak and pineapple skewers to desired doneness. To serve, slice steak thinly on the diagonal; serve with pineapple.

Freeze uncooked chicken, beef or pork cutlets with marinade in freezer bags. After thawing overnight in the fridge or picnic cooler, meat can go right into the skillet or onto the grill for a savory meal.

Anna's Easy Summer Marinade

Makes 4 servings

1/4 c. lemon juice
1/2 c. extra-virgin olive oil
1/4 c. fresh parsley, minced
1/4 c. fresh basil, minced
3 cloves garlic, minced

1/2 t. red pepper flakes
1/2 t. kosher salt
1/2 t. pepper
fresh dill, oregano and cilantro
   to taste, minced

In a bowl, whisk together all ingredients. Use immediately.

Serving tip:

Add 1-1/2 to 2 pounds beef, pork, chicken or seafood to a large plastic zipping bag. Pour marinade over top, turning to coat. Seal bag; refrigerate for 2 hours or overnight, turning occasionally. Drain, discarding marinade. Grill, bake or fry as desired. Marinade may also be used with vegetables.

Everyone loves a picnic and you don't need to head to
the park to have one. Even if you don't have a deck or
a patio, colorful blankets spread on the lawn (or in the
living room!) are fun for everyone.

Grilled Chicken Marinade

Serves 4 to 6

1/4 c. lemon juice
2 T. olive oil
2 cloves garlic, minced

1/2 t. dried oregano
1/2 t. dry mustard
salt to taste

Mix together all ingredients. Use immediately or refrigerate until ready to use.

Serving tip:

Flatten 1-1/2 to 2 pounds boneless, skinless chicken breasts slightly; arrange in a shallow glass dish. Pour marinade over chicken, turning to coat well. Cover and refrigerate for 2 to 8 hours. Drain, discarding marinade. Grill chicken as desired.

For the most mouthwatering marinated chops and steaks, pat the meat dry with a paper towel after draining off the marinade. Then sprinkle on any seasonings before placing it on the hot grill.

Karen's Soy Beef Marinade

Makes 4 to 6 servings

3/4 c. oil
1/4 c. soy sauce
3 T. honey or sugar
2 T. cider vinegar or lemon juice

1/2 t. ground ginger
1 clove garlic, minced,
   or 1/4 t. garlic salt
Optional: 1 green onion, chopped

Whisk together all ingredients. Use immediately or refrigerate until ready to use.

Serving tip:

Cut 2 pounds favorite beef steak into serving-size pieces; place in a large plastic zipping bag. Pour marinade over steak; seal bag and turn to coat well. Refrigerate for 4 to 5 hours, turning occasionally. Drain, discarding marinade. Grill steak as desired.

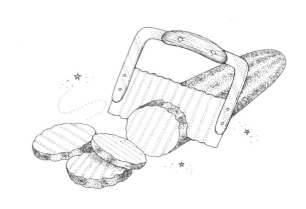

Add extra texture to fresh veggies for snack trays...
use a crinkle cutter to cut them into slices and sticks.

Country Market Salad Marinade *Makes 4 servings*

3/4 c. canola oil
1/2 c. white vinegar
1 T. fresh basil, chopped

1 T. fresh tarragon, chopped
1 T. salt
1/4 t. pepper

Combine all ingredients; whisk until well blended and salt is dissolved. Use immediately.

Serving tip:

In a large salad bowl, combine 4 sliced ripe tomatoes, one peeled and sliced cucumber and 1/2 sliced onion; pour marinade over top. Cover and refrigerate for 5 to 6 hours. To serve, use a slotted spoon to arrange vegetables over chopped romaine or iceberg lettuce. Serve with remaining marinade, if desired.

Need to peel tomatoes in a hurry? Simply drop them into boiling water, then submerge them in cold water... the skins will slip right off.

Garden-Fresh Catsup

Makes 2, one-quart jars

3 lbs. ripe tomatoes, peeled
  and chopped
1 onion, peeled and diced
1/2 c. vinegar
1/2 c. sugar
1 t. paprika
1 t. salt

1 t. pepper
1/2 t. nutmeg
1/4 t. ground cloves
1 T. chili sauce
2 one-quart wide-mouth canning
  jars, sterilized

Mix together all ingredients in a large stockpot. Bring to a boil over medium heat. Reduce heat to medium-low; simmer for 20 minutes, stirring often. Remove from heat; let cool. Ladle into jars, leaving 1/8-inch headspace. Wipe rims; add lids. Store in refrigerator up to 2 weeks.

Show off your relish in Mom's antique cut-glass compote.
When washing cut glass, add a little white vinegar to
the rinse water...the glass will really shine!

Grandma's Fresh Relish

Makes 6 to 8 servings

1 ripe tomato, diced
1 green pepper, diced
3 green onions, diced,
    both white and green parts

1 cucumber, peeled and diced
1-1/2 T. sugar
salt and pepper to taste

Combine all ingredients in a bowl; stir well. Cover and chill. The vegetables will create a wonderful juice. Keep refrigerated 3 to 5 days.

Serving tip:

Serve relish with hot dogs or brats, or as a chilled salsa with chips.

Serve up some warm soft pretzels with Farmhouse Honey Mustard. Twist strips of refrigerated bread stick dough into pretzel shapes and place on an ungreased baking sheet. Brush with beaten egg white, sprinkle with coarse salt and bake as directed.

Farmhouse Honey Mustard   *Makes about 3/4 cup*

1/4 c. mayonnaise
1/4 c. Dijon mustard
1/4 c. honey

1 T. mustard
1 T. white vinegar
1/8 t. paprika

Whisk together all ingredients in a small bowl. Cover and store in the refrigerator for up to one week.

Serving tip:

Spread on sandwiches, drizzle over salads or spoon into a bowl for dipping chicken tenders...yum!

Pick up a stack of vintage plastic burger baskets. Lined with crisp paper napkins, they're still such fun for serving burgers and fries...clean-up after dinner is a snap too!

Special Hamburger Sauce

1 c. mayonnaise
1/3 c. creamy French salad
   dressing
1/4 c. sweet pickle relish

1 T. sugar
1 t. dried, minced onion
salt and pepper to taste

Combine all ingredients in a bowl; stir well. Cover and refrigerate up to one week.

Serving tip:
Spoon sauce over grilled or pan-fried burgers.

Dining outdoors on a hot, humid day? Keep salt
free-flowing...simply add a few grains
of rice to the shaker.

Steak Onion Butter

1/4 c. butter, softened
1/4 c. Bermuda onion, grated
1/4 c. fresh parsley, minced
1 t. Worcestershire sauce

1/2 t. salt
1/2 t. pepper
1/4 t. dry mustard

Blend all ingredients in a small bowl. Use immediately or cover and refrigerate.

Serving tip:
Dollop butter onto grilled steaks just before serving.

Recycle with style! Label colorful metal buckets
with stick-on vinyl letters.

Lemony Sage Mayonnaise

Makes about 2 cups

2 c. mayonnaise
1/2 c. fresh sage, finely chopped,
   or 3 T. dried sage
2 T. lemon juice

1 T. plus 1 t. lemon zest
1 T. garlic, minced
1 t. pepper

Whisk together all ingredients. Cover and store in the refrigerator for up to one week.

Serving tip:

Top deli-style sandwiches with this spread...it's packed with flavor!

Using recycled jars to store homemade rubs and sauces?
Remove stubborn labels and inked expiration dates with
a swab of rubbing alcohol.

Mediterranean Herb Rub

Makes one cup

1/3 c. grated Parmesan cheese
1/3 c. pepper
2 T. dried thyme
2 T. dried rosemary

2 T. dried basil
1 t. garlic powder
1 t. salt

Mix together Parmesan cheese and pepper; add remaining ingredients and stir well. If a finer texture is desired, process in a food processor. Store in a covered jar up to one week.

Serving tip:

Rub over chicken or beef; grill as desired.

If it's easy and flavorful, it's a favorite!
Rubs are a great way to add flavor to
your grilled veggies.

JoAnn's Jamaican-Me-Hungry Jerk Rub

*Makes about
2-1/2 tablespoons*

2 t. sugar
1-1/2 t. onion powder
1-1/2 t. dried thyme
1 t. allspice
1 t. pepper

1/2 to 1 t. cayenne pepper
1/2 t. salt
1/4 t. nutmeg
1/8 t. ground cloves

Combine all ingredients in an airtight container; shake to mix. Cover and store up to one week.

Serving tip:

Sprinkle over meat of your choice; rub it in with your fingers. Grill as desired.

Pack some favorite seasonings or sauces into a barbecue gift bag for a much-appreciated hostess surprise! Cut 2 back pockets from a pair of old blue jeans, arrange on the front of a white gift bag and secure with hot glue. Slip a sassy red bandanna in one pocket and a few recipe cards in the other.

All-Purpose Barbecue Rub *Makes about 2/3 cup*

1/4 c. brown sugar, packed
1 T. chili powder
1 T. paprika
1 T. kosher salt
2 t. garlic powder
2 t. onion powder

1 t. ground celery seed
1 t. ground cumin
1 t. dried oregano
1 t. pepper
1/2 t. cayenne pepper

Mix together all ingredients; place in a shaker container with a lid.

Serving tip:

Sprinkle generously on chicken, pork or beef or fish before grilling, baking or slow cooking.

Fill whimsical retro salt & pepper shakers with rubs and salt blends for gifts for any time of the year.
Don't forget to attach a favorite recipe.

Dad's Famous Steak Rub

Makes about 2 cups

3/4 c. paprika
1/4 c. sugar
1/4 c. salt
1/4 c. pepper

2 T. chili powder
2 T. garlic powder
2 T. onion powder
2 t. cayenne pepper

Combine all ingredients; mix well. Store in an airtight container.

Serving tip:
Sprinkle over steaks before grilling...it really packs a flavorful punch. Great with roasts too!

Here's a tasty apple coleslaw that goes well with pork.
Simply toss together a large bag of coleslaw mix, a cored and
chopped Granny Smith apple, 1/2 cup mayonnaise and
1/2 cup plain Greek yogurt. Scrumptious!

Spicy Rubbed Pork Tenderloin   *Makes 6 to 8 servings*

1 to 3 T. chili powder, to taste
1 t. salt
1 t. pepper

1/4 t. ground ginger
1/4 t. dried thyme
1/4 t. dry mustard

Mix together all spices in a bowl. Use immediately or store in a plastic zipping bag.

Serving tip:

Rub desired amount of spice mixture over both sides of a one-pound pork tenderloin fillet. Wrap tightly in aluminum foil; refrigerate for 8 hours to overnight. Remove foil. Grill on an oiled grate over medium-high heat to desired doneness, turning once or twice, about 15 to 20 minutes. Remove to a platter; let stand for 10 minutes. Slice thinly and serve with natural juices.

A vintage wooden soft-drink crate makes
a handy picnic carrier.

Roy's Steak Seasoning

Makes 7 tablespoons

1 T. dried, minced onion
4 T. kosher salt
1 T. coarse pepper

1 T. granulated garlic
1 T. paprika

In a food processor, finely chop onion to the same consistency as other ingredients. Combine onion and remaining ingredients in a jar; cover and shake to mix well.

Serving tip:

Sprinkle to taste over steak, burgers, pork loin or chicken while grilling.

Chicken breasts are a favorite in recipes, but give chicken thighs a try too! They're juicier and more flavorful...perfect for grilling.

Vickie's Chicken Rub

3 T. paprika
1 T. garlic powder
1 T. ground cumin
1 T. ground ginger

2 t. salt
1-1/2 t. cinnamon
1 t. cayenne pepper

Combine all ingredients in a jar; cover and shake well to mix.

Serving tip:

Use about one tablespoon of mixture for each pound of chicken breast; rub well into the meat. Grill or bake as desired.

A mortar & pestle is useful for crushing and mixing dried herbs and spice seeds to your own taste. If you don't have one, a brief whirl in a mini food processor will do the trick.

Secret BBQ Dry Rub

Makes 4 servings

1/2 c. brown sugar, packed
1 T. chili powder
1 T. salt
1 t. onion powder

1 t. garlic powder
1/2 t. dried thyme
1/2 t. cayenne pepper
1/2 t. seafood seasoning

Mix together brown sugar and seasonings; store in an airtight container.

Serving tip:

Rub over both sides of 2 to 3 pounds southern-style pork ribs. Let stand at least 10 minutes, or cover and refrigerate up to 6 hours. Grill ribs as desired, basting with your favorite barbecue sauce.

Get together with neighbors and head to the local park for a dinner picnic. The kids play, the grown-ups talk and everyone eats great homemade food...just like the good ol' days.

St. Louis-Style Rib Rub

Serves 6

1/2 c. sugar
2 T. seasoning salt
2 T. sweet paprika
2 t. chili powder

2 t. dry mustard
1 t. garlic powder
1 t. pepper
1/8 t. cayenne pepper

Mix together all ingredients. Use immediately, or store in an airtight container.

Serving tip:

Apply evenly over 2 pounds of pork ribs. Place ribs in a large plastic zipping bag; seal and refrigerate overnight. Grill as desired.

A special gift for a favorite cook...tuck a jar of
Spicy Cajun Rub into the pocket of a new ruffled apron!

Spicy Cajun Rub

Makes about 2/3 cup

1/4 c. paprika
4 t. onion powder
4 t. garlic powder
4 t. cayenne pepper
4 t. salt

1 T. white pepper
1 t. pepper
2 t. dried thyme
2 t. dried oregano

Combine all ingredients in a bowl; mix well. Store in an airtight container.

Serving tip:

Sprinkle generously on pork chops or pork tenderloin before grilling or roasting. Excellent with fish too...sprinkle over fillets before pan-frying.

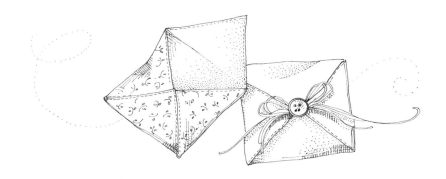

A sampler seasoning pouch makes a clever gift for cooks.
Lay a square dinner napkin flat, fold 3 corners to the center and
handstitch together, forming an envelope. Fill it with several bags
of seasoning mix, then fold the fourth corner down to close.
Add a button to close, or wrap a ribbon around to secure.

Cooking-Out Steak Rub

Makes about 1-1/2 cups

1/2 c. brown sugar, packed
1/4 c. sugar
2 T. chili powder
2 T. paprika
2 T. dry mustard
2 T. garlic powder

2 T. dried, minced onion
1 T. dried oregano
1 T. dried thyme
1 T. dried basil
1 T. cayenne pepper

Combine all ingredients; mix well. Store in an airtight container.

Serving tip:
Sprinkle over steaks; grill as desired.

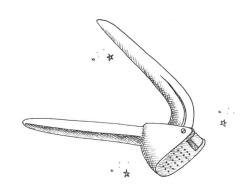

To peel garlic easily, crush the clove with the side of a knife.
For really speedy mincing, use a garlic press.

Garlic, Salt & Paprika Rub

Makes about 2 cups

26-oz. pkg. salt
1 whole bulb garlic, peeled

3 to 4 T. paprika, divided

Pour salt into a large bowl. Press garlic directly into salt so all of the liquid is added to the rub. Do not mash. Add paprika by spoonfuls until mixture is a medium-brown color, mixing between spoonfuls. Store in a tightly covered container.

Serving tip:

Rub onto brisket, beef roast, turkey or chicken; cover and refrigerate for one to 2 days. Grill or roast as desired. Excellent on baked potatoes and vegetables too.

Keep green onions fresh longer by storing them bulb-ends down in a half-full glass of water in the refrigerator. Change the water every few days.

Lori's Fresh Salsa

Makes about 4 cups

4-oz. can diced green chiles
2 14-1/2 oz. cans petite diced
   tomatoes, divided
1 to 2 jalapeño peppers, seeded
   and chopped
1/3 c. fresh cilantro, chopped

1/2 white onion, chopped
6 green onions, chopped
1 to 2 wedges lime
1/4 t. red pepper flakes
salt and pepper to taste

In a blender, combine green chiles and one can tomatoes with juice.
Process for about 5 seconds; do not overblend. Transfer to a bowl; add
second can of tomatoes with juice, jalapeños, cilantro and onions. Mix
lightly. Squeeze in lime juice; add seasonings. Cover and chill for one hour
before serving. Keep refrigerated up to one week.

Serving tip:

Scrumptious for snacking with tortilla chips...try this on scrambled eggs,
baked potatoes and salads too.

How can you tell when a pineapple is ripe? Just check the base...
if it's green, it's not ripe yet. If it's orange or mushy,
it's too ripe. But if it's yellow and bright, it's just right.

Fresh Pineapple Salsa

Makes 2 cups

2 c. fresh pineapple, diced
2 green onions, chopped
1/4 c. green pepper, diced
1/4 c. fresh cilantro, minced

4 t. lime juice
1/8 t. cayenne pepper
1/8 t. salt

Combine all ingredients in a small bowl. Mix well; cover and chill until serving time.

Serving tip:

In a small bowl, combine 2 tablespoons lime juice and one tablespoon canola oil; brush over 2 pounds tilapia fillets. Arrange fillets on a grill pan; season lightly with salt and pepper. Cook over medium heat, turning once, for 6 to 8 minutes, until fish flakes easily with a fork. Serve with Fresh Pineapple Salsa.

Almost any fresh veggie can be added to a favorite salsa recipe. Try stirring in chopped peppers, green onions, minced garlic and sweet corn.

Quick & Easy Summer Salsa

Makes 2-1/2 to 3 cups

10 roma tomatoes, chopped
1 c. fresh cilantro, chopped
1/2 c. red onion, chopped

1 T. vinegar
1/2 c. olive oil
juice of 2 key limes

Combine all ingredients except chips in a bowl; stir to blend. Refrigerate until chilled.

Serving tip:

Serve as a topping for grilled chicken or your favorite Mexican dish, or enjoy with tortilla chips.

When buying fresh fruits & veggies at the farmers' market, keep them farm-fresh by packing them in a cooler in your car.

Celebration Fruit Salsa

1 c. strawberries, hulled and chopped
1 orange, peeled and finely chopped
2 kiwi, peeled and finely chopped
1/2 fresh pineapple, peeled and finely chopped, or 8-oz. can crushed pineapple, drained
1/4 c. green onion, thinly sliced
1/4 c. green or yellow pepper, finely chopped
1 T. lime or lemon juice
1 jalapeño pepper, seeded and chopped

Combine all ingredients except garnish and tortilla chips in a bowl; stir well. Refrigerate until chilled.

Serving tip:
Serve with grilled pork or chicken...delicious with cinnamon tortilla chips too.

Mild, medium or spicy...salsa is scrumptious on so many foods.
Jazz up plain burgers or hot dogs with a dollop of salsa
instead of catsup. Turn eggs sunny-side up into huevos
rancheros with a dollop of salsa and a sprinkling of cheese.
Salsa can even be used as a fresh sauce for pasta!

Fresh Cali Salsa

Serves 4

6 roma tomatoes, chopped
2 bunches fresh cilantro, coarsely
  chopped
1 red onion, chopped

3 jalapeño peppers, diced
juice of 1 lime
1/8 t. coarse salt

Combine all ingredients in a bowl; toss to mix well. Cover and refrigerate for several hours to combine flavors.

Serving tip:

Delicious on just about anything, including grilled steak and sandwiches.

Homemade Ranch Dressing is more than a salad dressing...
it's a yummy dip for carrots, celery stalks and
other fresh veggies.

Homemade Ranch Dressing   *Makes about 1-1/2 cups*

1 c. mayonnaise
1/2 c. sour cream
1/2 t. dried chives
1/2 t. dried parsley
1/2 t. dill weed

1/4 t. garlic powder
1/4 t. onion powder
1/8 t. salt
1/8 t. pepper

Whisk all ingredients together in a medium bowl. Cover and chill for at least 30 minutes, so flavors can blend. Keep refrigerated.

Serving tip:

Serve on your favorite chopped or wedge lettuce salad...scrumptious for dipping too.

When frying bacon, it's easy to prepare a few extra slices
to tuck into the fridge. Combine with juicy slices of
sun-ripened tomato, frilly lettuce and creamy mayonnaise for
a fresh BLT sandwich...tomorrow's lunch is ready in a jiffy!

Charlotte's Hot Endive Dressing

Serves 4 to 6

1/3 c. cider vinegar
3/4 c. water
1 lb. bacon
2 eggs, beaten

1 c. sugar
2 T. cornstarch
2 T. mustard

Combine vinegar and water; set aside. In a skillet over medium heat, cook bacon until crisp. Remove bacon from skillet, reserving drippings. Crumble bacon into bits and set aside. Add eggs to drippings in skillet over low heat; cook and stir until scrambled. Add vinegar mixture to skillet; stir until well blended. Mix together sugar, cornstarch and mustard; add to skillet.

Serving tip:

Chop one head fresh endive and add to hot mixture in skillet. Cook until softened, about 5 minutes; serve warm. This dressing is delicious spooned over mashed potatoes too.

A vintage wooden salad bowl is a terrific thrift-shop find.
To restore the bowl's glowing finish, sand lightly inside and out
with fine sandpaper. Rub a little vegetable oil over the bowl and
let stand overnight, then wipe off any excess oil in the morning.
It will look like new!

Lemony Caesar Dressing

1/2 c. olive oil	1 t. Dijon mustard
3 T. lemon juice	1/2 t. salt
2 cloves garlic, minced	1/8 t. pepper

Blend all ingredients until smooth. Cover and keep refrigerated.

Serving tip:
Drizzle this dressing over grilled or baked chicken and fish...garnish with lemon wedges.

Give homemade salad dressings as gifts, packed in
sweet vintage bottles tied up with a simple herb bouquet.

Garlic Vinaigrette

1/3 c. oil
1/3 c. white wine vinegar
2 cloves garlic, minced

1 T. sugar
1/2 t. salt
1/8 t. pepper

Combine all ingredients in a jar with a tight-fitting lid. Secure lid; shake vigorously to blend. Will stay fresh in the refrigerator for up to 2 weeks.

Serving tip:

Drizzle over fresh greens for a wonderful tossed salad. Makes a great chicken marinade too.

INDEX

INDEX

Our Story

Back in 1984, we were next-door neighbors raising our families in the little town of Delaware, Ohio. Two moms with small children, we were looking for a way to do what we loved and stay home with the kids too. We had always shared a love of home cooking and making memories with family & friends and so, after many a conversation over the backyard fence, **Gooseberry Patch** was born.

We put together our first catalog at our kitchen tables, enlisting the help of our loved ones wherever we could. From that very first mailing, we found an immediate connection with many of our customers and it wasn't long before we began receiving letters, photos and recipes from these new friends. In 1992, we put together our very first cookbook, compiled from hundreds of these recipes and, the rest, as they say, is history.

Hard to believe it's been over 35 years since those kitchen-table days! From that original little **Gooseberry Patch** family, we've grown to include an amazing group of creative folks who love cooking, decorating and creating as much as we do. Today, we're best known for our homestyle, family-friendly cookbooks, now recognized as national bestsellers.

One thing's for sure, we couldn't have done it without our friends all across the country. Each year, we're honored to turn thousands of your recipes into our collectible cookbooks. Our hope is that each book captures the stories and heart of all of you who have shared with us. Whether you've been with us since the beginning or are just discovering us, welcome to the **Gooseberry Patch** family!

Visit our website anytime
www.gooseberrypatch.com

Jo Ann & Vickie

Email

1·800·854·6673